Oda
a una
cebolla

Textos de
Alexandria Giardino

Ilustraciones de
Felícita Sala

Traducción de
Juan Fernando Merino

PANAMERICANA
EDITORIAL
Colombia • México • Perú

Giardino, Alexandria.
      Oda a una cebolla Pablo Neruda y su musa / Alexandria
Giardino ; ilustraciones Felicita Sala ; traducción Juan
Fernando Merino. -- Editor Alejandra Sanabria Zambrano. --Bogotá :
Panamericana Editorial, 2020.
      36 páginas : ilustraciones ; 29 cm. -- (Rayuela)
      Título original : Ode to An Onion.
      ISBN 978-958-30-6002-1
      1. Cuentos infantiles americanos 2. Personajes - Cuentos infantiles 3. Libros
ilustrados para niños. I. Sala, Felicita, ilustradora. II. Merino, Juan Fernando,
traductor. III. Sanabria Zambrano, Alejandra, editora. IV. Tít. V. Serie.
I813.6 cd 22 ed.
A1654458

                  CEP-Banco de la República-Biblioteca Luis Ángel Arango

Primera edición en Panamericana Editorial Ltda.,
enero de 2020
Textos © 2018 Alexandria Giardino
Ilustraciones © 2018 Felicita Sala
Fotografía publicada con el permiso del Archivo
Fotográfico Fundación Pablo Neruda
Poema "Oda a la cebolla",
Odas elementales © 1954,
Pablo Neruda y Fundación Pablo Neruda

Publicado por primera vez en inglés en 2018
por Cameron Kids, un sello de Cameron + Company. Inc.
Título original en inglés: *Ode To An Onion*
Publicado en acuerdo con Harry N. Abrams. Inc.
© 2019 Panamericana Editorial Ltda.
Calle 12 No. 34-30, Tel.: (57 1) 3649000
www.panamericanaeditorial.com
Tienda virtual: www.panamericanaeditorial.com.co
Bogotá D. C., Colombia

Editor
Panamericana Editorial Ltda.
Edición
Alejandra Sanabria Zambrano
Ilustraciones
Felicita Sala
Traducción del inglés
Juan Fernando Merino
Diagramación
Jairo Toro

ISBN 978-958-30-6002-1

Impreso por Panamericana Formas e Impresos S. A.
Calle 65 No. 95-28, Tels.: (57 1) 4302110 - 4300355. Fax: (57 1) 2763008
Bogotá D. C., Colombia
Quien solo actúa como impresor.
Impreso en Colombia - *Printed in Colombia*

Para Nicolas, cuya energía y espíritu
son tan Grandes
como los de Pablo.

—A. G.

Para James.

—F. S.

Pablo trabajaba con ahínco,
escribiendo un largo y triste poema.
Su pluma iba y venía.
Las páginas se amontonaban.

El reloj dio las doce.

Pablo se incorporó de un salto. Iba a llegar tarde a almorzar con su amiga Matilde.
Se pasó el peine por el cabello y deseó no tener un aspecto tan sombrío.

A Matilde le gustaba reír.
Tenía una sonrisa tan amplia como un estero
en invierno.
Pablo trató de ocultar su expresión taciturna
detrás de un ramo de amapolas.

—No hay tiempo para la tristeza —dijo Matilde
mientras llenaba un jarrón con agua—. ¡Ven!
Necesito tu ayuda con el almuerzo.

—Incluso en las cosas más sencillas —dijo Matilde, secándose las lágrimas.

—Como las cebollas —añadió Pablo.

—¡Deberías escribir sobre eso!
—dijo Matilde, riéndose.

—Luminosa cebolla —proclamó Pablo, levantando el bulbo—. ¡Las cosas tristes siempre me han hecho llorar, pero tú me has hecho llorar de alegría! Es por ello que te celebraré como solo un poeta puede hacerlo. ¡Con una oda!

—¡Pero primero comamos!
—dijo Matilde.

Sobre Pablo & Matilde

Pablo Neruda nació en Chile en 1904. Comenzó a escribir poesía cuando era un niño y, a los diecinueve años, se hizo famoso por un libro de poemas de amor. Como Pablo era una persona muy sensible, que siempre se daba cuenta de las injusticias, usó el poder de sus poemas para describir lo que veía, esperando que sus lectores se conmovieran y anhelaran hacer que el mundo fuese mejor. Después de publicar muchos libros de excelsos poemas, Pablo comenzó a componer odas sencillas porque quería escribir sobre las cosas comunes, cotidianas y felices, como los calcetines y los caldos. Por esa época, conoció a Matilde Urrutia en un concierto realizado en un parque en Santiago, la capital de Chile. Matilde era una cantante de música folclórica que se reía fácilmente y con frecuencia. Pablo se deleitaba con su espíritu alegre y pronto se enamoraron. Construyeron juntos un hogar, en el cual Matilde se ocupaba de un amplio y copioso jardín, y Pablo trabajaba en una mesa elaborada con maderas que el mar arrastraba a la playa, escribiendo odas sobre todas las cosas, desde el maíz y las alcachofas hasta, sí, ¡hasta las cebollas!

Entre las obras más famosas de Pablo se encuentran *Odas elementales, Canto general* y *Veinte poemas de amor y una canción desesperada.* También escribió un libro de memorias llamado *Confieso que he vivido.* Esta historia, *Oda a una cebolla,* se inspiró en el poema de Pablo "Oda a la cebolla" y en las memorias de Matilde, *Mi vida con Pablo Neruda.*

Oda a la cebolla

Pablo Neruda

Cebolla,
luminosa redoma,
pétalo a pétalo
se formó tu hermosura,
escamas de cristal te acrecentaron
y en el secreto de la tierra oscura
se redondeó tu vientre de rocío.
Bajo la tierra
fue el milagro
y cuando apareció
tu torpe tallo verde,
y nacieron
tus hojas como espadas en el huerto,
la tierra acumuló su poderío
mostrando tu desnuda transparencia,
y como en Afrodita el mar remoto
duplicó la magnolia
levantando sus senos,
la tierra
así te hizo,
cebolla,
clara como un planeta,
y destinada
a relucir,
constelación constante,
redonda rosa de agua,
sobre
la mesa
de las pobres gentes.
Generosa
deshaces
tu globo de frescura
en la consumación
ferviente de la olla,
y el jirón de cristal
al calor encendido del aceite
se transforma en rizada pluma de oro.

También recordaré cómo fecunda
tu influencia el amor de la ensalada,
y parece que el cielo contribuye
dándote fina forma de granizo
a celebrar tu claridad picada
sobre los hemisferios de un tomate.
Pero al alcance
de las manos del pueblo,
regada con aceite,
espolvoreada
con un poco de sal,
matas el hambre
del jornalero en el duro camino.
Estrella de los pobres,
hada madrina
envuelta
en delicado
papel, sales del suelo,
eterna, intacta, pura
como semilla de astro,
y al cortarte
el cuchillo en la cocina
sube la única lágrima
sin pena.
Nos hiciste llorar sin afligirnos.
Yo cuanto existe celebré, cebolla,
pero para mí eres
más hermosa que un ave
de plumas cegadoras,
eres para mis ojos
globo celeste, copa de platino,
baile inmóvil
de anémona nevada
y vive la fragancia de la tierra
en tu naturaleza cristalina.

"Oda a la cebolla", *Odas elementales*
© 1954, Pablo Neruda y Fundación Pablo Neruda

Alexandría Giardino

es escritora y traductora del español. Vive con
su familia en el norte de California. Este es su
primer álbum ilustrado.

Felícita Sala

es ilustradora autodidacta. Ha trabajado en
varios libros ilustrados. Creció en Australia
y ahora vive en Roma con su familia.

Most of the books listed below can be used with young children, ages three through eight. With younger children in that range, you may want to condense or paraphrase the text in some of the books. You can make decisions about this on an individual class basis. Some books are chapter books; these should be used only with grades one through three.

Ackerman, Karen. *Song and Dance Man.* New York: Scholastic, Inc., 1988.

A grandpa entertains his grandchildren with his old song and dance routines.

Adler, David. *A Picture Book of Martin Luther King, Jr.* New York: Scholastic, Inc., 1989.

The short text presents the main events in King's childhood and his achievements as an adult. This is a good choice for younger children.

Aiello, Barbara, and Jeffrey Shulman. *Business Is Looking Up.* Frederick, Md.: Twenty-First Century Books, Inc., 1988.

In this chapter book, visually impaired Renaldo sets up a greeting card business for stepfamilies.

_____. *Hometown Hero.* Frederick, Md.: Twenty-First Century Books, Inc., 1989.

This chapter book presents Scott, who is learning how to cope with his asthma while befriending a homeless person.

_____. *It's Your Turn at Bat.* Frederick, Md.: Twenty-First Century Books, Inc., 1988.

In this chapter book, Mark, a fifth-grader with cerebral palsy, is manager for his baseball team. When money for the team jerseys is lost, Mark tries to find a solution.

_____. *A Portrait of Me.* Frederick, Md.: Twenty-First Century Books, Inc., 1989.

In this chapter book, Christine has to work to learn to cope with her diabetes and to accept her place in her Greek-American family.

_____. *Secrets Aren't Always for Keeps.* Frederick, Md.: Twenty-First Century Books, Inc., 1988.

In this chapter book, Kay has to decide whether to tell her pen pal that she has a learning disability.

_____. *Trick or Treat or Trouble.* Frederick, Md.: Twenty-First Century Books, Inc., 1989.

In this chapter book, Brian, who has epilepsy, and his friends learn what things are scary and not so scary on Halloween.

Althea. *I Use a Wheelchair.* Cambridge, Great Britain: Dinosaur Publications, 1983.

A girl confined to a wheelchair talks about the ways in which she copes with her life in a wheelchair. The language has some "Britishisms" that are interesting for children to hear.

Anderson, Joan. *Pioneer Children of Appalachia.* New York: Clarion Books, 1986.

This book uses photographs (taken at a living history museum) and text to show what life was like in Appalachia in the early 1800s.

Austin, James. *Christopher Columbus.* Edina, Minn.: Abdo & Daughters, 1990.

This book details the life of Columbus from early years until his death, including information on all his voyages to the Americas.

Blaine, Marge. *The Terrible Thing That Happened at Our House.* New York: Scholastic, Inc., 1975.

When a little girl's mom goes back to teaching, lots of family routines change, and adjustments have to be made by everyone in the family.

Brenner, Barbara. *Wagon Wheels.* New York: Harper & Row, 1978.

In this true story, an African-American pioneer family makes a life for themselves in Kansas after the Civil War.

Briggs, Raymond. *Jim and the Beanstalk.* New York: Coward-McCann Inc., 1970.

Jim climbs a beanstalk, meets and aids an aging giant.

Cameron, Ann. *The Stories Julian Tells*. New York: Bullseye Books, 1981.

Julian gets into trouble with some tall tales, but gets out of trouble with the help of a sympathetic dad and his own ingenuity. An African-American family is portrayed.

Church, Vivian. *Colors Around Me*. Chicago: Afro-Am Publishing Company, Inc., 1971.

This book is a good book for preschool children; it contains strong pictures of African-American children of all different shades of color; the words give brief positive associations to the colors black and brown.

Clifton, Lucille. *My Friend Jacob*. New York: E.P. Dutton, 1980.

Sam and his neighbor, Jacob, have a strong friendship despite Jacob's intellectual limitations.

Climo, Shirley. *The Egyptian Cinderella*. New York: Thomas Y. Crowell, 1989.

Rhodopis, a slave girl, is left behind when servant girls go to watch the Pharaoh hold court. Eventually her red slipper is found by the Pharaoh, who seeks its owner to be his queen.

Cohen, Barbara. *Molly's Pilgrim*. New York: Lothrop, Lee & Shepard Books, 1983.

A Russian-Jewish immigrant, Molly is teased by classmates. When Molly's mother makes Molly a Pilgrim doll that looks like a Russian immigrant, Molly's class comes to appreciate a broader definition of the word *pilgrim*.

Cohen, Miriam. *See You Tomorrow, Charles*. New York: Greenwillow Books, 1983.

Charles, who is blind, is able to guide himself and Maria out of a darkened room near the school playground.

Cooney, Barbara. *Miss Rumphius*. New York: Puffin Books, 1982.

Alice wants to follow in her grandfather's footsteps by seeing faraway places, living by the sea, and making the world more beautiful.

Crowder, Jack. *Tonibah and the Rainbow.* Bernalillo, N.M.: Upper Strata Ink, Inc., 1986.

Written in Navajo and English, the story tells of a present-day Navajo family whose hogan burns down and must be rebuilt.

deKay, James. *Meet Martin Luther King, Jr.* New York: Random House, 1969.

This book details King's life and includes photographs of King at various times in his life.

Ellis, Veronica. *Afro-Bets First Book about Africa.* Orange, N.J.: Just Us Books, 1989.

This book presents some basic facts of African history in an easy-to-understand style.

Feelings, Muriel. *Jambo Means Hello.* New York: Dial Books for Young Readers, 1974.

This book is an alphabetical introduction to the Swahili language and East African life.

_____. *Mojo Means One.* New York: Dial Books for Young Readers, 1971.

This book is an introduction to counting in Swahili and to East African life.

Ferris, Jeri. *Walking the Road to Freedom: A Story About Sojourner Truth.* Minneapolis: Carolrhoda Books, Inc., 1988.

This chapter book details Sojourner Truth's career as an orator for abolition of slavery and for women's suffrage.

Flournoy, Valerie. *The Patchwork Quilt.* New York: Dial Books for Young Readers, 1985.

When her grandmother becomes ill, Tanya works to finish a quilt that tells their family story through its varied patches. An African-American family is portrayed.

Friedman, Ina. *How My Parents Learned to Eat.* Boston: Houghton Mifflin Co., 1984.

A Japanese girl and American sailor try to learn the other's way of eating, with pleasant results.

Gray, Nigel. *A Country Far Away*. New York: Orchard Books, 1988.

The minimal text compliments the illustrations in this story of two boys, one African and one American, who wake, sleep, play, eat, and share in family life on opposite sides of the world.

Greenfield, *Eloise*. Darlene Methuen. 1980.

Darlene has to wait for her mom to pick her up; she keeps busy even though she is in a wheelchair.

_____. *Honey, I Love*. New York: Harper & Row, 1978.

This book contains wonderfully warm poems about friends, family, and important things; the poems speak with a child's voice.

Haskins, Jim. *Count Your Way Through Japan*. Minneapolis: Carolrhoda Books, Inc., 1989.

Photos and text show how to count in Japanese, as well as some fundamentals of Japanese life. Similar books are available for Korea, Canada, Mexico, China, and the Arab world.

Havill, Juanita. *Jamaica's Find*. Boston: Houghton Mifflin Co., 1986.

Jamaica finds a stuffed dog at the park and wrestles with whether to keep it or turn it in to the lost-and-found. An African-American family is portrayed.

Hazen, Barbara. *Why Are People Different?* Racine, Wis.: Western Publishing Co., 1985.

In this book about an African-American family, Terry thinks no one at his new school likes him. His grandma helps him when she remembers having similar feelings. Terry finally makes friends with some fellow students who are also musicians.

Heide, Florence Parry, and Judith Heide Gilliland. *The Day of Ahmed's Secret*. New York: Lothrop, Lee & Shepard Books, 1990.

Ahmed's job is to deliver canisters of gas throughout Cairo. Ahmed has an enjoyment of the city and the added excitement of a secret to share with his family at the end of the day.

Hoffman, Mary. *Amazing Grace*. New York: Dial Books for Young Readers, 1991.

Grace loves to act out stories. She sets her sights on being Peter Pan for her class play, despite her classmates' notion that an African-American girl can't be Peter Pan.

Hudson, Cheryl, and Bernette Ford. *Bright Eyes, Brown Skin.* Orange, N.J:. Just Us Books, 1990.

Pictures of children in a preschool setting accompany a poem.

Ikuhara, Yoshiyuki. *Children of the World: Bolivia*. Milwaukee: Gareth Stevens, Inc., 1988.

Many photos and an excellent text combine to present a thorough picture of the life of Porfirio Esteban, an eleven-year-old Aymara Indian. The book also has pictures and information on Bolivia itself.

Jassem, Kate. *Sacajawea*. Mahwah, N.J.: Troll Associates, 1978.

This chapter book tells the story of Sacajawea's kidnapping, life with her trapper husband, and travels with the Lewis and Clark expedition.

Jenness, Aylette. *Families*. Boston: Houghton Mifflin, 1988.

This book contains photographs and short biographies of children in diverse family settings.

Johnston, Tony. *The Quilt Story*. New York: G.P. Putnam's Sons, 1985.

A pioneer girl keeps warm with a quilt made by her mother; the quilt is rediscovered years later and reclaimed by another mother and daughter.

Keats, Ezra Jack. *Peter's Chair*. New York: Harper & Row, 1967.

Peter (an African-American boy) has to come to terms with the addition of a baby sister to his family.

Kessel, Joyce. *Squanto and the First Thanksgiving*. Minneapolis: Carolrhoda Books, Inc., 1983.

This book tells the story of Squanto, who, after his early years as a slave, returns to the Plymouth area to teach the Pilgrims farming and hunting techniques suitable to the area.

Klingel, Cindy. *We the People: Harriet Tubman.* Mankato, Minn. Creative Education, 1987.

One of a series of books about famous people (women, Native Americans, war heroes, frontierspeople, explorers), this book presents the accomplishments of Tubman: her work on the Underground Railroad, as a nurse, as a scout and spy in the Civil War, and as an advocate for the poor.

Levine, Ellen. *I Hate English.* New York: Scholastic, Inc., 1989.

Mei Mei, who has come to New York from Hong Kong, resists speaking English until she meets an understanding teacher.

Lowery, Linda. *Martin Luther King Day.* Minneapolis: Carolrhoda Books, Inc., 1987.

This book offers an explanation of the holiday in honor of Martin Luther King, Jr., by presenting the major accomplishments and legacy of the man.

MacLachan, Patricia. *Through Grandpa's Eyes.* New York: Harper & Row, 1980.

John loves to visit his grandpa. Though blind, Grandpa shows John his own ways of seeing.

Martin, Bill, and Bill Archambault. *Knots on a Counting Rope.* Henry Holt & Co., 1989.

"Tell me the story again," Boy says to Grandfather. Grandfather tells the story of how Boy has learned well despite his blindness. This is a story about a Native American family.

McKenna, Nancy Durrell. *A Zulu Family.* Minneapolis: Lerner Publications, 1986.

This book shows the life of eleven-year-old Busisiwe, a Zulu girl in South Africa. It also describes the life of her family and that of relatives, the difficulties of living under apartheid, and the family's pride in its Zulu heritage.

McKissack, Patricia. *Flossie and the Fox.* New York: Dial Books for Young Readers, 1986.

A troublesome fox meets his match in bright Flossie, who insists on proof that he really is a fox. Flossie is African-American.

Merriam, Eve. *Daddies at Work.* New York: Little Simon, 1989.

This book contains multi-ethnic drawings of daddies at work at their parenting jobs and at a cross-section of other jobs.

_____. *Mommies at Work.* New York: Little Simon, 1989.

This book contains multiethnic drawings of mommies at work at their parenting jobs and at a cross section of other jobs.

Miles, Miska. *Annie and the Old One.* Boston: Atlantic Monthly Press, 1971.

Annie struggles to accept the idea that her grandmother will die when the rug her mother is weaving is finished.

Milne, A. A. *The House at Pooh Corner.* New York: Dutton, 1988.

Winnie-the-Pooh and Christopher Robin continue their adventures with Rabbit, Eeyore, Piglet, Tigger, Kanga, and Roo.

Monjo, F.N. *The Drinking Gourd.* New York: Harper & Row, 1970.

Young Tommy and his father help slaves escape to Canada via the Underground Railroad. The story may appeal to younger readers, but the concepts relating to an underground railroad are more appropriate for second- and third-graders.

Morris, Ann. *Bread, Bread, Bread.* New York: Lothrop, Lee & Shepard Books, 1989.

Different breads from many cultures are depicted in photographs.

_____. *Hats, Hats, Hats.* New York: Lothrop, Lee & Shepard Books, 1989.

Another photographic panorama; this time the photographs are of different hats from around the world.

_____. *Loving.* New York: Lothrop, Lee & Shepard Books, 1990.

A rich variety of cultures is shown in photos that depict ways of loving all around the world.

Munsch, Robert. *The Paper Bag Princess.* Toronto: Annick Press, 1980.

Elizabeth is set to marry Ronald until a dragon kidnaps him. Elizabeth tricks the dragon, rescues Ronald, and decides not to marry him.

Musgrove, Margaret. *Ashanti to Zulu.* New York: Dial Books for Young Readers, 1976.

This strikingly illustrated book is an alphabetic presentation of twenty-six tribes of Africa with salient points about each tribe.

Ney, Stephanie. *Jo, Flo and Yolanda.* Chapel Hill, N.C.: Lollipop Power Books, 1973.

These Latino triplets have some things in common and some definite differences.

Peterson, Jeanne. *I Have a Sister; My Sister is Deaf.* New York: Harper & Row, 1977.

A deaf girl's sister tells how she does many of the usual things children enjoy even though her methods are different at times.

Quinsey, Mary Beth. *Why Does That Man Have Such a Big Nose?* Seattle: Parenting Press, 1986.

This book seeks to answer the natural curiosity children have about people who look different.

Rabe, Berniece. *The Balancing Girl.* New York: E.P. Dutton, 1981.

Although Margaret uses a wheelchair, she is a careful builder and makes a structure that helps raise money for a school fair.

Ringgold, Faith. *Tar Beach.* New York: Crown Publishers Inc., 1991.

In her dreams, a young girl flies above her Harlem home, feeling empowered to change the unfairness in her family's life. The story comes from a story quilt created by the author, which is now in the Guggenheim Museum.

Rogers, Alison. *Luke Has Asthma, Too.* Burlington, Vt.: Waterfront Books, 1987.

A younger boy learning to accept his asthma is encouraged by an older boy, Luke, who shares the condition.

Sabin, Louis. *Narcissa Whitman.* Mahwah, N.J.: Troll Associates, 1982.

The book tells of Whitman's childhood, her dream of going west, and her eventual settlement in Oregon.

Say, Allen. *The Bicycle Man.* New York: Scholastic, Inc., 1982.

Japanese schoolchildren having their sports day are joined by two American soldiers, one of whose performance on a bicycle bridges the postwar awkwardness between the children and their military occupiers.

Seeger, Pete. *Abiyoyo.* New York: Scholastic, Inc., 1963.

The story, adapted by Seeger, is based on a South African folktale about a giant who is defeated by a song and a magic wand.

Simon, Norma. *All Kinds of Families.* Chicago: Albert Whitman & Co., 1975.

This book uses appealing text and drawings to show the diversity of families and their activities.

Spier, Peter. *People.* Garden City, N.Y.: Doubleday & Co., Inc., 1980.

Rich illustrations and text combine to present a panorama of how people are the same and how they are different.

Stanek, Muriel. *I Speak English for My Mom.* Niles, Ill.: Albert Whitman & Co., 1990.

A young Mexican-American girl must translate for her mother, who speaks only Spanish.

Steelsmith, Shari. *Elizabeth Blackwell.* Seattle: Parenting Press, 1987.

This book tells Blackwell's story in first-person narrative: her determination to become a doctor, her setbacks, and her triumphs.

Stevenson, Robert Louis. *My Shadow.* New York: G. P. Putnam's Sons, 1990.

A wonderful potpourri of children and their shadows illustrate this version of the poem, "My Shadow."

Surat, Michele Maria. *Angel Child, Dragon Child*. New York: Scholastic, Inc., 1983.

Ut, a Vietnamese child, has difficulty being accepted in her American school. Ut and her particular tormentor, Raymond, finally come to appreciate one another and work together to raise money to bring Ut's mother to the United States from Vietnam. This book is based on a true story.

Taylor, Sydney. *Danny Loves a Holiday*. New York: E.P. Dutton, 1980.

In each chapter, Danny celebrates a different Jewish holiday, often with a special Danny twist.

Turner, Glennette. *Take a Walk in Their Shoes*. New York: Cobblestone Books, 1989.

This book contains biographical vignettes of fourteen noted African Americans. Chapters include brief skits of incidents in the lives of these individuals; these can be performed by elementary students.

Ward, Leila. *I Am Eyes/NiMacho*. New York: Greenwillow Books, 1978.

A young Kenyan boy enjoys the sights of the early morning.

Waters, Kate. *Sarah Morton's Day*. New York: Scholastic, Inc., 1989.

A day in the life of a real Pilgrim girl is told in text and through photographs taken at Plimouth Plantation.

_____, and Madeline Slovenz-Low. *Lion Dancer*. New York: Scholastic, Inc., 1990.

Through photographs and text, the reader sees the Wan family prepare and celebrate Chinese New Year in New York City.

Weil, Lisa. *I, Christopher Columbus*. New York: Atheneum Children's Books, 1983.

This book tells the story of the life of Columbus in first-person narrative. The drawings are somewhat cartoonlike.

Williams, Karen. *Galimoto*. New York: Lothrop, Lee & Shepard Books, 1990.

Overcoming obstacles and the doubts of his elders, a young African boy gathers the materials necessary to make a prized toy car.

Williams, Vera B. *A Chair for My Mother*. New York: Scholastic, Inc., 1982.

A Hispanic grandmother, mother, and daughter save coins in a big jar to buy a comfortable chair.

_____. *Something Special for Me*. New York: Mulberry Books, 1983.

This time the coins in the big jar are for a birthday present; Rosa searches for the perfect present for herself.

_____. *Music, Music for Everyone*. New York: Mulberry Books, 1984.

In the third book in this trilogy, Rosa and her friends form a band to make some money to help pay for Grandmother's medical expenses.

Wilson, Christopher. *A Treasure Hunt*. Washington, D.C.: United States Department of Health, Education, and Welfare, 1980.

This book shows a series of active older adults who help some children complete a treasure hunt.

Yarbrough, Camille. *Cornrows*. New York: Coward-McCann Inc., 1979.

While a brother and sister have their hair braided, their grandmother and mother tell of the strong traditions of their African homeland.

Young, Ed. *Lon Po Po*. New York: Scholastic, Inc., 1990.

In this Red Riding Hood story from China, three girls outwit the wolf while their mother is gone.

Young, Robert. *Christopher Columbus and His Voyage to the New World*. Englewood Cliffs, N.J.: Silver Press, 1990.

This book details the early life and first voyage of Columbus.

Zaslavsky, Claudia. *Count on Your Fingers African Style*. New York: Harper & Row, 1989.

This book is a survey of how African tribes count.